Saying Goodbye

Cecil Murphey and Gary Roe

PAINTINGS BY *Michal Sparks*

HARVEST HOUSE PUBLISHERS
EUGENE, OREGON

D0443336

Saying Goodbye

Text copyright © 2013 by Cecil Murphey and Gary Roe
Artwork copyright © 2013 by Michal Sparks

Published by Harvest House Publishers
Eugene, Oregon 97402
www.harvesthousepublishers.com

ISBN 978-0-7369-5059-6

> Mr. Gifford B. Bowne II
> Indigo Gates
> 1 Pegasus Drive
> Colts Neck, NJ 07722
> (732) 577-9333

Design and production by Garborg Design Works, Savage, Minnesota

Special thanks to Gail Smith for her suggestions in the section titled "Dos and Don'ts to Prepare Yourself."

All Scripture quotations are from the *Holy Bible*, New Living Translation, copyright © 1996, 2004. Used by permission of Tyndale House Publishers, Inc., Wheaton, IL 60189 USA. All rights reserved.

To Shirley.
With love,
Cec

To E. L. Roe for
being the dad he
was and to Don
and Sue Wills
for stepping in as
my new parents.
Where would I be
without you?
Thank you,
Gary Roe

CONTENTS

INTRODUCTION

by Cecil Murphey

How do we look into the eyes of someone we love and realize that person will die soon? Some stay away when they hear words like "terminal" or "dying." Others try to behave as if it's just an option clause someone inserted in an important document.

Death is real.

We hurt when someone we love reaches that final stage of life here on earth.

You may be facing the loss of someone you love. Whether you've gotten along well or argued often, as long as the other one lives, you have hope for a healthy relationship. But death puts an end to possibilities and dreams.

❧

I was a pastor for fourteen years and grieved with many families when they faced loss. I also worked part-time as a volunteer hospital chaplain for ten years. Gary was also a full-time pastor for fourteen years and currently serves as a hospice chaplain and interim pastor for a small congregation.

Both of us have had to say goodbye to those we loved. Both of us have been with others as they prepared for the loss of someone they loved.

We share with you what we've learned from our own grief and healing experiences as well as the experiences of others.

Prepare Yourself

FROM GARY

"What would you tell someone whose loved one is dying?" I asked Sandra, who had lost her mother two years previously.

"Prepare yourself," she answered. "I knew what to expect, and that made a big difference for me." She said that hospice gave her a family handbook that outlined the process a typical patient and family go through. "I read and reread it. Knowing what would probably happen next took away the anxiety and fear."

That was excellent advice because most of us don't handle uncertainty well. If we prepare for what may happen, we can cope better, even if we don't have to experience everything we learn. Though this can be unnerving, I urge family members to face what lies ahead. As painful as it may be, accept the reality of the situation.

Education and information lead us out of denial. We learn to accept things as they are, rather than as we wish them to be.

"Don't waste a moment," Sandra added. "Live so that you have no regrets. You can never have that time back. My mom's final months are some of the most memorable times of my life. I have no regrets."

No regrets.

Someone said, "When it comes to death, cultures are death-accepting, death-defying, or death-denying." Ours is death-denying. We pretend that death won't happen, so we don't prepare. We miss good things that take place in the dying process and end up with many regrets.

Sandra said it in simple terms: Say what we need to say. Do what we need to do. Express thanks. Affirm. Forgive. Ask forgiveness. Make amends.

No regrets.

When I was fifteen years old, my father was in the hospital for a week following a massive heart attack. He never regained consciousness. I lived at the hospital that week, even though I saw him only twice daily for one-hour periods.

I sat beside his bed during each of those hour sessions and talked about whatever was on my mind and inside my heart. I had yelled at him two days before his collapse. I apologized for that and other things in which I had been wrong. The one thing I said repeatedly was, "I love you." I wish I had said it more often before that week.

On Dad's final night, the nurse stopped me in the hallway. "Have you said everything you wanted to say?" she asked. "He's probably listening. Hearing is the last thing to go."

Her words stunned me. I had been talking for *me*, and she helped me see I was also talking for *him*. I went into his room and again spoke nonstop for an hour.

Dad passed away at three o'clock the next morning.

If that nurse hadn't explained the value of talking to Dad, I wouldn't have understood. We can meet our loved ones where they are and make their last hours meaningful for them and for us.

The more we know, the more power we have over fear's ability to overwhelm us. The more we resist spending our energy on anxious thoughts, the more available we are to express love. I think of the words:

"Love has no fear, because perfect love expels all fear" (1 John 4:18).

Like Sandra I have no regrets, and I view death differently now. I understand the process. Death is no longer an enemy; death is a part of life.

Making ourselves ready may be painful now, but preparing ourselves makes it less painful afterward.

I've Made Mistakes

FROM CEC

"I've made lots of mistakes in my life," Myrtle said. She's been an invalid for four years, and her dementia steadily progresses. Although once talkative, now she rarely follows a conversation or responds to questions.

I nodded at her words, but she wasn't finished. "I've made lots of mistakes in my life. I just can't remember them anymore."

She grinned and so did I.

How aware was Myrtle when she said those words? I have no idea, but I know the effect they had on me. Like Myrtle I've made mistakes. I've spoken mean, hate-filled words that I'd like to take back. I've done things that make me wince when I remember them. That doesn't make me unique; that probably describes most of us.

As we quietly sit beside those we love and realize that we're slowly losing them, life tends to slow down. Perhaps this is a good time to peacefully examine our hearts, prepare to say goodbye, and even face our failures.

At times like this, we focus on what we might have done, should have done, or could have done better. No matter how much we care, we tend to feel guilty. We're too focused on ourselves and our own needs. We've been too emotionally insulated to accept the pain of someone we love.

We remember those difficult moments. Possibly

we remember too many of those moments. Most of the actions were minor, and few were life changing. To us, however, they're still marks of failure. Wrongdoings. Sins. Errors of judgment. Regardless of what we call them, they are mistakes. And we torture ourselves by going back, reliving the events, and telling ourselves what we wish we had done differently.

Eventually, though, we admit to ourselves that this does no good. The past is over, and it's time to let go of our failures. We can learn from the two simple statements Myrtle made, "I've made lots of mistakes in my life. I just can't remember them anymore."

I ponder her words almost every day.

That's the way I want to live. With those words ringing inside my heart, I do the best I can—not perfectly and not always lovingly. As I care for my loved one, I make mistakes, if not today, then certainly by tomorrow. I may say too much or too little. I'm likely to say something inappropriate, lose patience, and make impossible demands of my loved one or myself.

Instead of wallowing in self-pity or self-disdain, I've decided that with God's help, I'm going to change. Life isn't about how many mistakes I've made or how bad they were.

DEAR GOD,
I'VE MADE
MANY, MANY
MISTAKES.
HELP ME TO
REMEMBER
THEM NO
LONGER.

It's about how I respond. I respond by telling God, "I'm sorry. Please forgive me." If there are others involved, I say to them, "Please forgive me." Finally, I say—sometimes repeatedly—to myself, "I forgive me."

Once I speak and accept those words, I'm ready to put them behind me. That's the difficult part, but I can do it.

A friend once said, "It's not what you *did*, but what you do next that really counts." For me that means I can't recast the past, but I can leave it in the past and move forward.

How will I know when I've forgiven myself? During my years in Kenya, I had a serious fallout with Bud, a senior missionary. When I returned to the States, I was still hurting because we hadn't resolved our differences. Eventually I wrote and apologized for my wrongdoing, and soon he did the same. Now I can't remember what we argued about.

I like the way the psalmist says it: "He has removed our sins as far from us as the east is from the west" (Psalm 103:12). I remind myself that God has taken my sins away. I dishonor God by remembering them.

As I prepare to say goodbye to someone I love, I don't want to focus on what I did wrong or how my loved one failed me. I want to remember the joyous times and relive the kind and thoughtful moments. If I can do that, I know I'll forget the bad times.

We can't undo our failures, but God has forgotten them. Why shouldn't we?

He Loves Me

FROM CEC

She was blind and elderly. Her cancer had progressed rapidly, and dementia had robbed her of all but about five words. Her only regular response came when someone sat beside her and sang. Sometimes she smiled. Other times she repeated one or two words.

On one visit, I began singing "Jesus Loves Me."

She turned her face toward me and listened intently. After I finished, she sat up in bed and smiled. Then she cried out, "He loves me! He loves me! He loves me!"

I didn't know what to say because I'd never heard her put more than two words together at a time. She continued staring into my face as if those blind eyes were able to gaze into my soul. The huge smile lingered.

"Yes, He surely does," I said.

She lay down again and almost immediately fell asleep with that smile on her face.

I've reflected on that visit because, as simple as it was, the impact was profound. I sang a simple song that almost every child who attends church school knows by heart. It's probably the first Christian song many of us learned. The melody is effortless and the words are uncomplicated.

The message is obvious, and it doesn't need a lengthy theological

explanation. No one misunderstands "Jesus loves me! This I know..." I read somewhere that Anna Warner wrote and recited the poem for a dying child. Two years later William Bradbury added the music and the chorus.

Maybe that's why the elderly woman responded—not because she was dying, which she was, but because of the straightforwardness of that timeless hymn. Despite dementia, blindness, and cancer, she still could grasp that uncomplicated message.

The meaning *is* simple. We can dismiss the song as childish, and perhaps some do, but the simple words and melody make the song powerful. They convey the one truth that any person in the world at any time can say: "Jesus loves me."

Jesus loves me!

Me!

The dying woman's humble words expressed that she was ready to meet the Savior who loves her.

As I spoke with her son, his eyes brightened before he said, "She's ready."

Tears filled his wife's eyes, and she said, "Now I can say goodbye and be at peace."

Saying goodbye can be the end of a long and painful ordeal, or it can be a time of peace.

Take Care of You

Sam was always a pleasure to visit even though his respiratory condition was worsening quickly, and he struggled to breathe most of the time. We focused on keeping him as comfortable as possible.

One day after we read the Bible together and prayed, he looked deeply into my eyes and said over the noise of his oxygen, "You watch yourself. Take care of you." Then he smiled and said, "You're no good to me if you don't."

I think of Jesus' words when asked to give the greatest commands. "'Love the Lord your God with all your heart, all your soul, and all your mind.' This is the first and greatest commandment. A second is equally

important: 'Love your neighbor as yourself'" (Matthew 22:37-39).

In that well-known passage, Jesus weds two commands. For Him they cannot be separated. Expressing genuine love for others is one way of expressing love for God. And taking good care of ourselves enables us to love others better.

Many of us have difficulty taking care of ourselves. When we're stressed, eating right, exercise, and our pursuit of a healthy lifestyle get bumped down a few notches. When the stress concerns a loved one who will soon die, we think, *I'm not important right now. I need to take care of my loved one. I'll take better care of myself later.*

That reminds me of the flight attendant's standard speech before the airplane takes off. It's the same on every airline. If the cabin loses pressure, oxygen masks will drop from the compartment above our heads. We are to put the mask over our nose and mouth and breathe deeply. If we're parents, we are to put the mask over our own nose and mouth first and then assist our children with their masks. Obviously a passed-out parent is no good to a suffocating child.

Yet it's a parent's first instinct to place that mask on the kid before putting their own on.

Sometimes we must resist doing the natural thing and do what feels unnatural. Taking care of yourself is one of the greatest gifts you can give your loved one. Imagine the stress and guilt it would potentially cause them if they knew you were injuring your health while caring for theirs? Resist wearing yourself down. Instead, get to know your limits, put the priority on taking care of you, and do a better job of taking care of the one you love.

⚘

My dad loved cars. He operated an auto salvage yard from the time he was sixteen until the day he died. I'll never forget what he said to me when he put the keys to my first car in my hand. "Take good care of her. Watch your speed. Keep gas in her. Get the oil changed regularly. And when she makes funny noises, get her checked out. You do that, and she'll get you where you need to go."

If we're going to care for our loved one well, we have to take care of ourselves. Watch our speed. Find a routine in the midst of the craziness and stick to it. Make sure we're eating, sleeping, and exercising well. If we get overwhelmed, maybe we need to take a break.

We need support too. Now more than ever, we need our friends. We need a support system to care for us as we care for another. We need

people to pray for us and make sure we take the best possible care of ourselves Though it would be nice to have these people automatically appear, most of the time we have to reach out.

It reminds me of the story of Moses and the Israelites in their first battle after leaving Egypt. As the battle starts, Moses watches from a hilltop with his staff raised. "As long as Moses held up the staff in his hand, the Israelites had the advantage. But whenever he dropped his hand, the Amalekites gained the advantage" (Exodus 17:11).

The longer the battle raged, the more tired the lawgiver became. Moses's brother, Aaron, and his nephew Hur found a rock for Moses to sit on. Then they stood on each side of Moses and held up his arms. Supported by those two men, Moses's arms stayed up until the Israelites defeated the enemy. Like Moses we need those who support our arms—people who will actively support us as we walk through the valley of the shadow of death with our loved one.

Your loved one depends on you. Don't lose your health while caring for her. Love her by loving yourself.

*If I want to care for my loved one,
I start by taking care of myself.*

Thanks for Going Through This with Me

FROM GARY

Leonard was talkative. Although his cancer was spreading rapidly, he had a smile on his face most of the time. He piloted his motorized scooter all over the assisted-living facility. A little American flag attached to the scooter waved behind his head. We always knew when Leonard was in the room.

One day I walked into his room to find him sitting in his scooter and looking out the window. I laid my hand on his shoulder. Neither of us said anything for several minutes. Finally he looked up at me and said, "Thanks for being present—for going through this with me."

I'm not sure we said anything more. Sometimes not much needs to be said. Just another person's presence is enough.

I think of Job, a man whose story most of us know. One day he loses his children and his property. Later his health is taken from him. Three good friends come to comfort him. When they see the intensity of his suffering, they're shocked. "When they saw Job from a distance, they scarcely recognized him. Wailing loudly, they tore their robes and threw dust into the air over their heads to show their grief. Then they sat on the ground with him for seven days and nights. No one said a word to Job, for they saw that his suffering was too great for words" (Job 2:12-13).

If only they had done nothing more.

After a week, Job speaks and expresses his grief. His friends feel compelled to respond. Instead of comforting Job, they try to explain his suffering. (And they got it wrong.)

Why would they do that?

I believe they tried to explain Job's situation because they were so uncomfortable with Job's pain. Instead of helping Job, they ended up causing him even more pain.

I tend to be like Job's friends. When I feel uncomfortable, I talk. I fill the air with words to help the hurting person feel better.

Our role is to love them and to be with them in their suffering—even when we're uncomfortable. Suffering can be difficult to watch. We feel powerless. And that leads to fear.

When I'm in pain, I want to know that I'm not alone. I'm not alone when someone is willing to be with me in my suffering.

❧

When I got out of the car at my dad's funeral, the pathway into the funeral home was packed on both sides with my high school friends. I locked eyes with many of them as I walked past. They didn't say a word. They were just there. And as I remember it more than thirty-five years later, I get a lump in my throat.

Your presence matters to your loved one. It may be the only way they sense God's loving presence.

My presence is the most powerful thing I have to offer. My presence says to my loved one, "I love you."

How Can I Affirm My Loved One?

FROM GARY

Sue was getting thinner. Although she was down to eighty pounds, she was all there mentally. She was spry in her behavior and quick with her words.

Sue grew up as the youngest of ten children on a farm. "I wanted only to be a wife and mother. And that's exactly what I was." She talked on and on about the farm and then meeting Walter, the love of her life. Walter had died just three months earlier. They'd been married seventy-five years.

About halfway through each of my visits, Sue would get discouraged. She'd been extremely active, but now she could barely walk from her recliner to the bathroom. She felt lost without Walter.

I believed Sue still had so much to give. She ministered to me when I was with her. She was a joy to be with. I consciously made a plan to affirm her during our visits. I said things like:

- You are always so encouraging. I leave here better off than when I walked in.
- Thank you for being such a faithful woman. You've been so steady and dependable.
- You were married for seventy-five years. That's amazing—a real accomplishment.
- I enjoy your humility. You're so open to hear whatever God might say to you.
- You smile no matter how you feel. And that says something about your heart. You have a good heart.

When I affirmed Sue, she blushed and talked with more energy. The light came back into her eyes.

Affirmation has great power. It's a conscious expression of love.

Though I've known Sue for only a few months, most of us have years of relationship with our loved ones and a long history full of "affirmation material." We can speak words of appreciation for who they are, affirm what they've done, and remind them of words they've spoken that have touched us deeply. Thank them—specifically and sincerely—often.

We can learn to pause each day and ask:

- What do I really appreciate about my loved one?
- How can I affirm my loved one?
- How can I encourage my loved one?

We all need to hear words of appreciation. I save those positive messages on my cell phone. In my email I keep a special file marked "encouragement." We can have a huge impact on our loved one's quality of life today by using affirming words.

True, it's hard to focus on giving love and appreciation to loved ones who are difficult, but it's important to do so even if our loved ones never reciprocate.

We build them up to make their burdens lighter and to prepare them to leave this world. When we speak, they may say, "Oh, that was nothing." Regardless, we need to tell them. We may assume they already know how we feel, but what if they don't? Isn't it better to say it again to make certain?

No one ever gets enough true affirmation. Everyone needs to be appreciated. We have the ability to speak the words that might make their last days better.

I can enhance my loved one's quality of life by expressing appreciation for who they are and what they've done.

Impart a Blessing to Me

FROM CEC

Larry spent almost every night after work at his father's bedside. That lasted almost three months before his father died of pancreatic cancer.

"That must have been a heavy ordeal for you," I said to him afterward.

"It was, but it was also a time of deep blessing." Larry talked for quite a while and spoke of the things he had learned. "Dad blessed me so much."

Even in his last days, the father was able to guide his son with suggestions about his business. That was part of the blessing Larry had mentioned. It's similar to the idea behind a blessing in the Old Testament.

In that context, a blessing was an *imparting* of knowledge or wisdom. It's what comes through the dimmed eyes of those who are near the end of their life's journey. It's what they leave behind for their heirs.

I wonder if too many leave this world with a storehouse of wisdom because they have no one to whom they can impart their insights. There's a tendency to sneer at the elderly. One time a new member of Alcoholics Anonymous, who was twenty-six, complained to me about his sponsor. "He's fifty-four. What does he know?"

My answer was, "More than you realize."

Because our loved ones are elderly or in pain, we tend to belittle their life experiences. They struggled through—and survived—many of the issues most of us have yet to face. Although they might have fared badly and made mistakes, they did survive.

We may not feel comfortable to say to our older loved one, "Bless me, Father," or "Bless me, Mother," but what if we thought of the blessing in the true biblical sense of the word?

For example many people don't understand the significance of the blessing Jacob stole from his brother Esau. As the older son, Esau was entitled to a double portion of everything. It was his birthright (Genesis 25:27-34). One day when Esau arrived home from a long day of hunting, Jacob took advantage of his brother's famished condition and convinced him to trade his birthright for food. But more important, Jacob later impersonated Esau to deceive his blind father into giving him the blessing, the double portion (Genesis 27:29).

The blessing to the ancients was more than a wish or a hope. They believed that the elderly could see the future, that their words were prophetic, and what they said would certainly happen.

After Esau learned of his brother's deception, he cried out to his father that Jacob had cheated him twice. "First he took my rights as the firstborn, and now he has stolen my blessing. Oh, haven't you saved even one blessing for me?" (Genesis 27:36b).

Here's Isaac's response: "I have made Jacob your master and have declared that all his brothers will be his servants. I have guaranteed him an abundance of grain and wine..." (Genesis 27:37).

If we asked our loved ones who are planning to leave this world, "Will you impart a blessing to me?" they probably wouldn't know what we meant. But if we asked the right questions, their answers might very well be worth carefully listening to.

Here are four questions we can ask:

- What is one thing you'd like me to remember?
- What makes a successful life?
- What one or two good things can you pass on about raising kids?
- What are the biggest lessons I need to learn in life?

If we ask simple questions about everyday living, their answers express what they have learned and give us a more objective frame of reference. For example, Nancy's mother was obese and took medications for a number of weight-induced diseases before she died at age fifty-two. She told her overweight teenaged daughter, "Take care of your body. I did everything wrong, and now I'm paying the price for it."

I met Nancy years ago at a fitness center, and she looked svelte and healthy. She received her mother's blessing.

My loved one may know things about life I need to learn. I will ask questions; I will listen to the answers.

I've Got Unfinished Business

FROM GARY

On one visit, Steven abruptly said, "I'm not ready to go. I've got things I need to take care of first." He talked about a broken marriage and an estranged son. He began to list the deep wounds in his life.

"I've been carrying these burdens too long and didn't know it," he said with tears in his eyes. "I held on to them, and they ended up controlling my life. I want to die free."

Our loved ones may not have the exact same problems as Steven, but many have unfinished business. In every relationship, misunderstandings, hurts, and resentments occur. We don't plan for them or want them, but they happen. Some people die without the closure they yearn for. Who wouldn't want to die free and at peace? Who wants to carry the weight of unfinished business through their final days?

Here are two things to ponder. First, we may need to forgive certain individuals. Do we have any resentments or wounds that need clearing that involve our loved one? Have we withheld our forgiveness?

Second, there may be others of whom we need to ask forgiveness. We may need to ask our loved one to forgive us. We might have to say, "If you hold anything against me... If you feel I've failed you..."

Here's something I do as a hospice chaplain. I invite patients to tell me the story of their lives beginning with childhood. Who were their best friends and worst enemies? What were the big defining events of their lives? As they tell their story, resentments often surface. Tears come. Sometimes anger bubbles up.

I listen, but I can't resolve their unfinished business. Allowing them to tell their stories can often be healing.

If we have unresolved issues with our loved one, let's face them. Ask yourself:

- Do I carry resentments toward her?
- Have I forgiven him?
- What part did I play in the hurts?
- Do I need to ask for forgiveness?

Make now—right now an opportunity to release the hurtful past. Asking and giving forgiveness is powerful and healing.

*Unfinished business
doesn't have to stay unfinished.
I can give, ask for, and
receive forgiveness.*

LORD, DO
I HAVE
UNFINISHED
BUSINESS WITH
MY LOVED ONE?
HAVE MERCY ON
ME AND HELP
ME RESOLVE IT.

DOES MY LOVED
ONE HAVE
UNFINISHED
BUSINESS?
HAVE MERCY
ON HIM AND
ALLOW ME TO
HELP HIM.

41

I Wish They Would Let Me Go

FROM CEC

"I didn't have time to grieve when my husband died," Maybelle said. "I had to keep my job because I had children to feed."

Her family had been her life, and now she was at the end. They surrounded her as she lay in a hospital bed in the living room of her oldest daughter's home. People stayed with her around the clock. Although exhausted, she pumped herself up for each interaction.

One day I asked the family to let me have some private time with Maybelle. After they closed the door, she let out a long, heavy sigh and said, "Thank goodness." She stared at the ceiling for several moments before she said, "I wish they would let me go."

I leaned forward and took her hand. "Have you ever told them that?"

She stared at me in momentary shock. "Well, no."

"Maybe they need you to give them permission to let you go."

A few days later, Maybelle's daughter said, "Mom just told us she was ready and asked us to let her go. We told her we loved her and that we would miss her."

Maybelle died that night.

Something happens to us when we love someone deeply. We begin to depend on them and build our world around them. If we're not careful, our *love* becomes more about what we think we need rather than our loved one's ultimate good.

"I wish they would let me go."

I wonder how many people have said those words to themselves because they couldn't share them with their family.

Sometimes we have to give people permission to let go; sometimes they have to give us permission to let go.

DEAR LOVING GOD, MAKE ME READY TO RELEASE MY LOVED ONE.

LET MY LOVE CENTER ON HER RATHER THAN ON MY NEED.

It's All Right to Die Now

FROM CEC

I can think of nothing more difficult than giving someone permission to die. You may have to do that. I've had to do it six times, of which two were with close relatives. It wasn't easy, but it was important.

My first experience was with Tommy who was in the intensive care unit at the hospital. The doctors told Tommy's family that there was no possibility for his recovery. He had delayed treatment, and the cancer had gone too far. The doctor had told Tommy he was going to die soon.

Although they weren't members of our congregation, they considered me their pastor. "Tommy keeps talking about getting better," his wife said. She and her daughter were distraught and didn't know how to respond.

"They've given him medication to ease the pain," the daughter said. "We want him to accept the truth."

"Our doctor said he should have died days ago," the wife said as she brushed away tears, "but he keeps holding on."

They weren't able to tell him to let go and surrender to death so they wanted me to do it. They waited while I went into the ICU to see him.

Tommy breathed laboriously as he listed the things he planned to do for his family when he got over this.

"They're going to be all right without you," I said.

"They need me." He started again to tell me what he planned.

I took Tommy's hand and leaned close so that he had to look directly at me. "They will be fine. It's all right for you to die now."

I repeated my words, "It's all right for you to die now." Then I added, "They're ready to say goodbye to you." I held Tommy's hand and kept his gaze until I knew he had truly heard me. "Will you let them come in and tell you goodbye?"

"You're sure?"

"Yes, I'm sure."

"Okay," he said.

"Will you let them come in and say goodbye?" I asked once more.

He nodded.

I told the family what happened. "Assure him that it's all right for him to die. If you can't say it that directly, say something like, 'It's okay to leave us,' but he needs your permission."

They did exactly what I asked. Tommy died soon afterward.

***

Ten years later, my older brother, Ray, was dying, and I went to see him. He sounded much like Tommy. I tried to comfort him and to tell him his five children and wife would be fine.

Like Tommy he insisted on telling me what he wanted to do for the family.

"Kate and the kids will be fine," I said. "You don't have to be responsible anymore." Before he could demur, I said, "It's all right to die. They love you, and they need to be able to say goodbye to you."

Ray didn't say anything more. I waited two or three minutes before I said, "I'm going to tell Katie to come in and say goodbye." He still said nothing.

I told Katie what to do.

The next day Ray died.

Katie called me and said, "I know it was the right thing. Ray died with a smile on his face."

***

In all six instances, it was as if the person couldn't surrender to death until they were assured that their loved ones would be all right.

If your loved one reacts similarly, you may have to be the one who reassures them. It probably won't be easy, but think of it as your final loving act. You are offering peace. You're allowing your loved one not to worry about *you*.

I can give permission for my loved one to leave us. I can assure my loved one that God will take care of us

Additional Information

Dos and Don'ts to Prepare Yourself

1. You are not the cheer giver. You are one who cares. Don't try to prevent your loved one from crying or talking about dying.

2. Don't try to push your loved one to face the facts. We all deal with issues differently.

3. Don't whisper around the dying person. You imply you have secrets you don't want the loved one to know.

4. If you feel like crying, cry. You don't need to protect your loved one. If you show no emotion, you may be giving the subtle message, "I don't care."

5. Be present with your loved one. The person needs you. Pay attention and listen carefully.

6. Avoid giving advice. Be there to love and express compassion.

7. Unless your loved one has dementia, don't make any plans without consulting with your loved one.

8. Talk to your loved one face-to-face and talk as an equal.

9. In your own way, make the person know you're willing to move to a deeper level when she is ready. But don't push.

10. Make this a time when you truly meet him. Apologize if you need to. Be as open and as caring as you can. If he has offended you, this isn't the time to ask for an apology. This is a time to forgive, love, and comfort.

11. Encourage her memories. Often a dying person wants to make sense out of life and to feel her life has mattered.

Comfort for Yourself and Your Family

1. Spend as much time as you can with your loved one. Make that a priority. You'll never be sorry for the time you spent with her.

2. They say we regret the things we didn't do more than the things we did do. Don't live with regret for failing to express love or compassion.

3. Talk to your loved one about his final wishes. If you are able, discuss arrangements for a funeral or a memorial service. Because of their grief after a death, family members are often in shock or traumatized by trying to make the significant decisions.

4. Make today count. Live in the moment with your loved one. Don't waste the time you have together by anticipating the pain and sadness to come. By enjoying your time with her now, you'll be better prepared to face loss.

5. Don't worry about what might happen. Jesus said, "Don't worry about tomorrow, for tomorrow will bring its own worries. Today's trouble is enough for today" (Matthew 6:34).

6. Each time you visit, tell your loved one how much you love and appreciate him. Cite specific experiences or expressions of their love and kindness. By doing that now, you can soften your grief because you've said nothing you will regret and you haven't left unsaid anything you wanted him to know.

7. Remind yourself that God is the God of all comfort. Read the Bible, especially those verses that bring you comfort. Many find comfort in reading and copying Psalms.

8. If appropriate, read the Bible to your loved one. Read portions that will bring comfort, such as Psalm 139, Revelation 20–21, 1 Thessalonians 4, or 1 Corinthians 15.

10. Talk with young members of the family about what is happening. Children certainly are aware of sadness and grief, but they may be confused if they don't understand what's happening.

11. Prepare children by talking truthfully with words appropriate for their age. If you feel ill-equipped to talk to them, ask a friend who is good with children to talk to them. The children's schoolteacher might be of help.

Let Others Comfort You in Your Grief

1. Your loved one's life touched many other lives. Invite friends to share something about your loved one at the funeral. You can receive comfort when you hear of your loved one's acts of kindness and compassion.

2. Be ready when someone asks, "Is there anything I can do?" If you sense the offer is sincere, allow that person to minister to you by helping you.

3. Let people know what is going on in your life. Tell your friends. You don't have to go into detail. Don't isolate yourself. You may need to remind yourself that there are individuals who care about you and want to know what you're going through. Being with loving friends reminds you that you're not alone in your grief.

4. Spend time with those who care about you. Ask them to pray for you. Go to lunch, see a movie, or take time to have a cup of coffee or a phone conversation with them. Share your experiences and listen to theirs.

5. Accept gifts, especially of food. See them as expressions of support. People care, and offering gifts is one way they express that concern.

6. Reach out to others who hurt or are in need. This may be difficult, but sometimes it helps to realize that others are also in pain. Pray for them. If possible, call or visit.

7. Reach out for help through the Internet. If your loved one was on Facebook or a social network, leave the profile page up after your loved one dies. Tell readers how they can connect with you or organizations to which they can give gifts in memory of your loved one.

Excellent Resources for a Grieving Heart

- Stephen Ministries (www.stephenministries.org)

- CaringBridge (www.caringbridge.org)

- GriefNet (www.griefnet.org)

- Good Grief (www.garyroe.com) is Gary Roe's website in which he offers inspirational and practical help for the grieving process.

- Your place of worship may have grief support groups or provide resources for you.

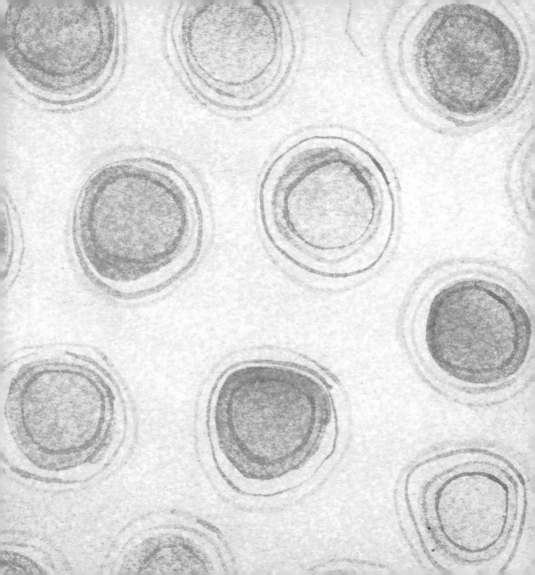

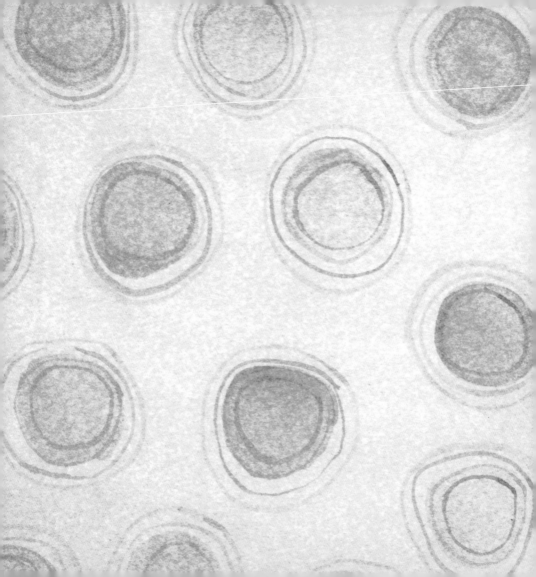